How to draw

CARS

Davina Claire Morgan

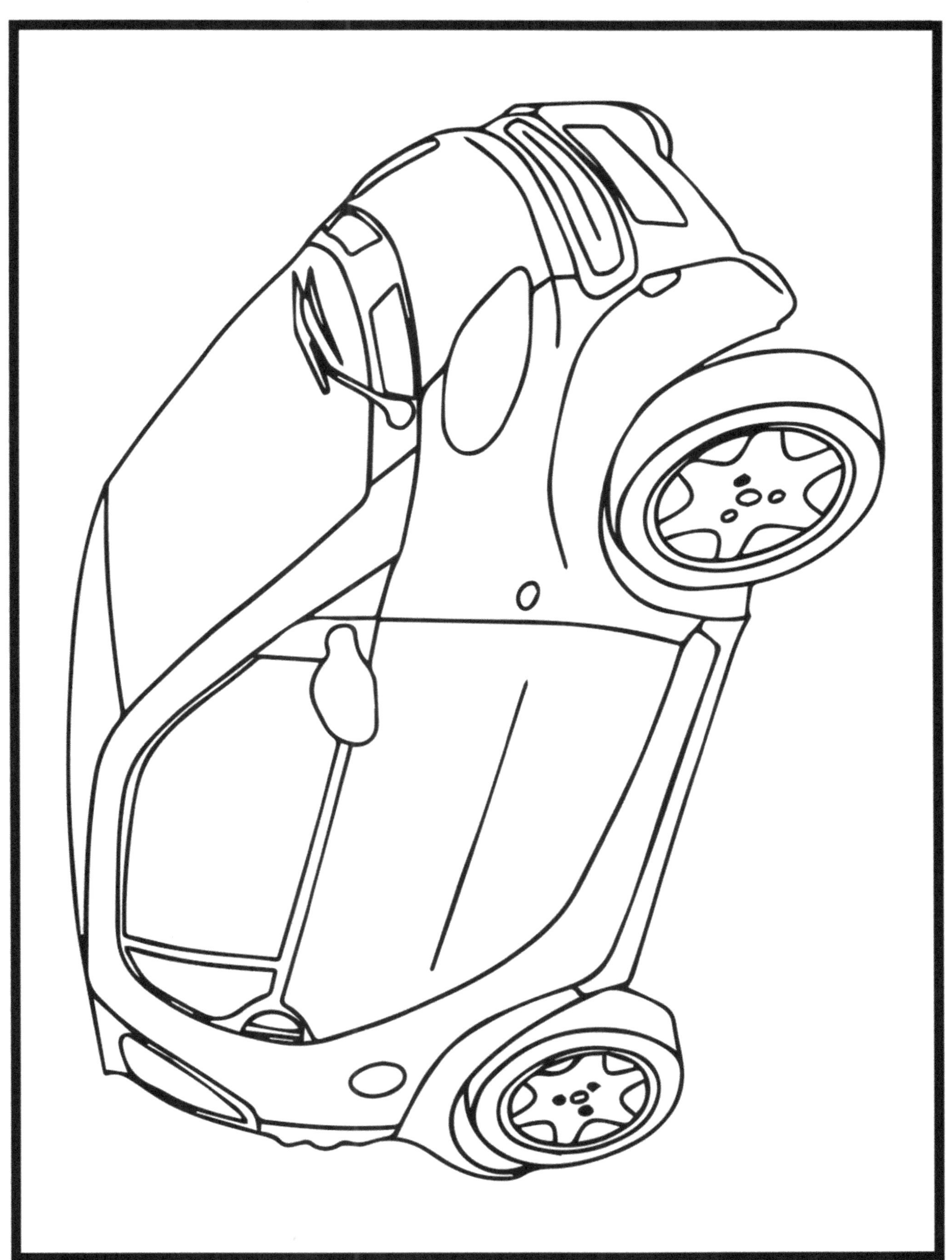

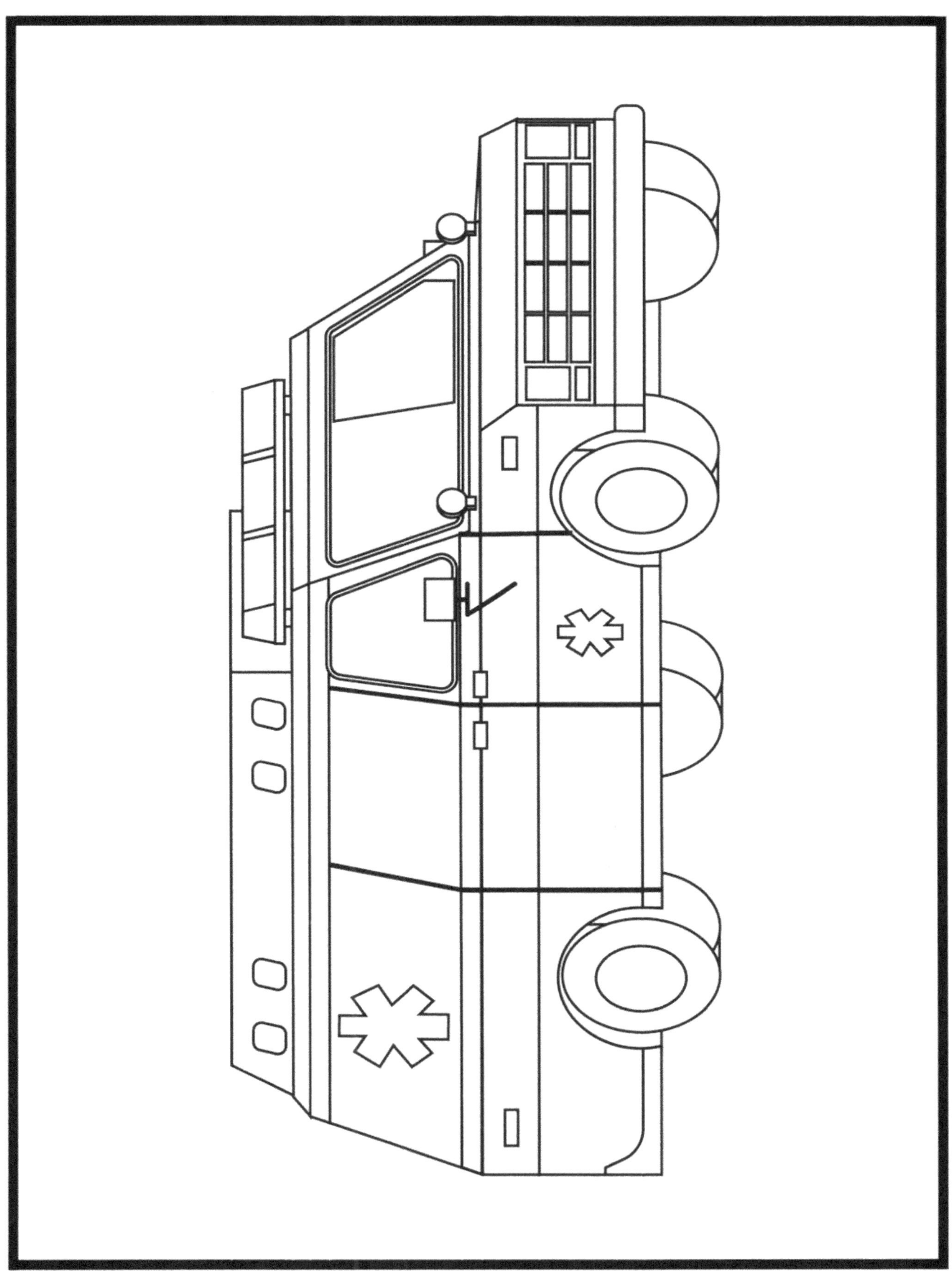

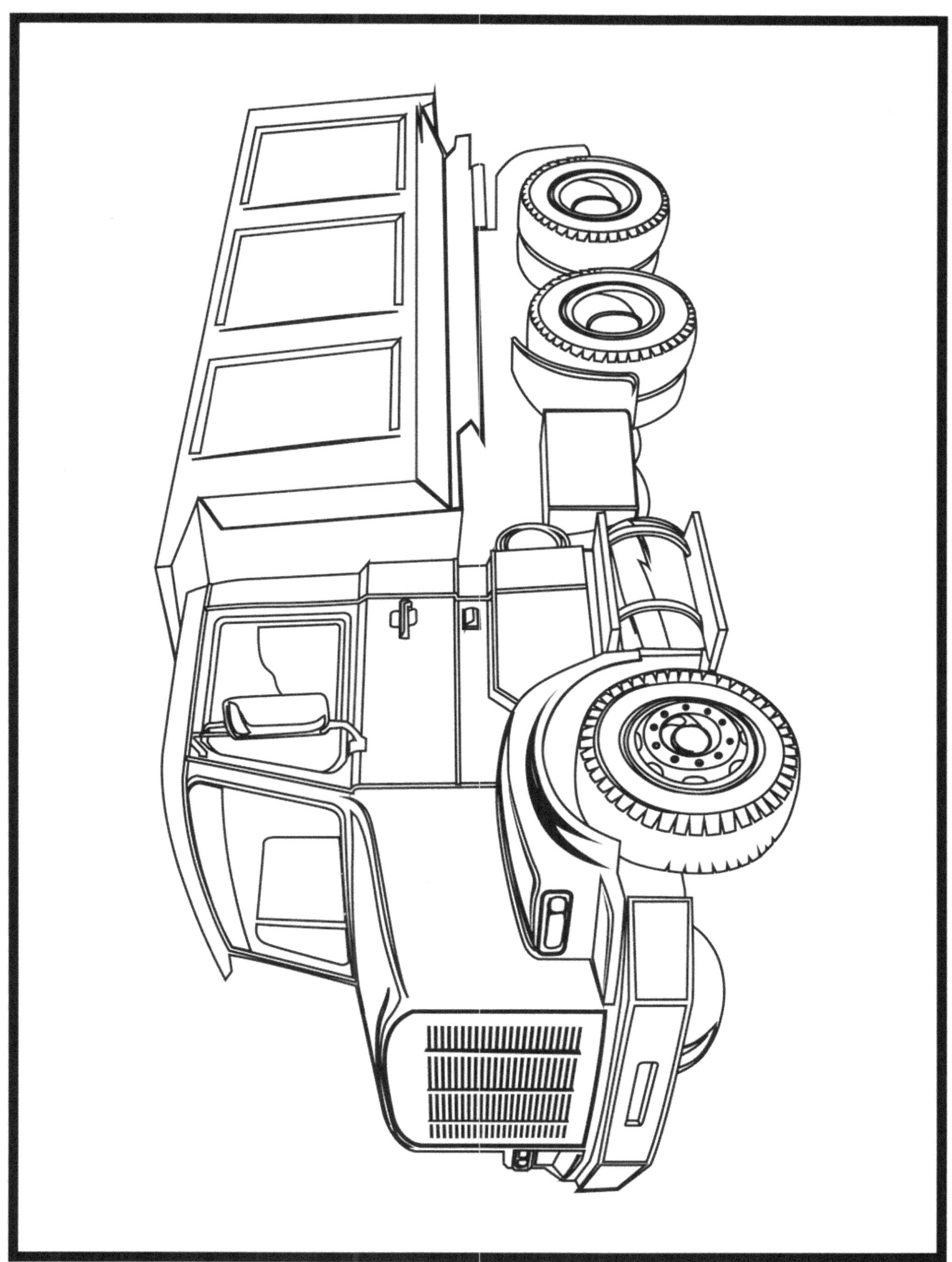

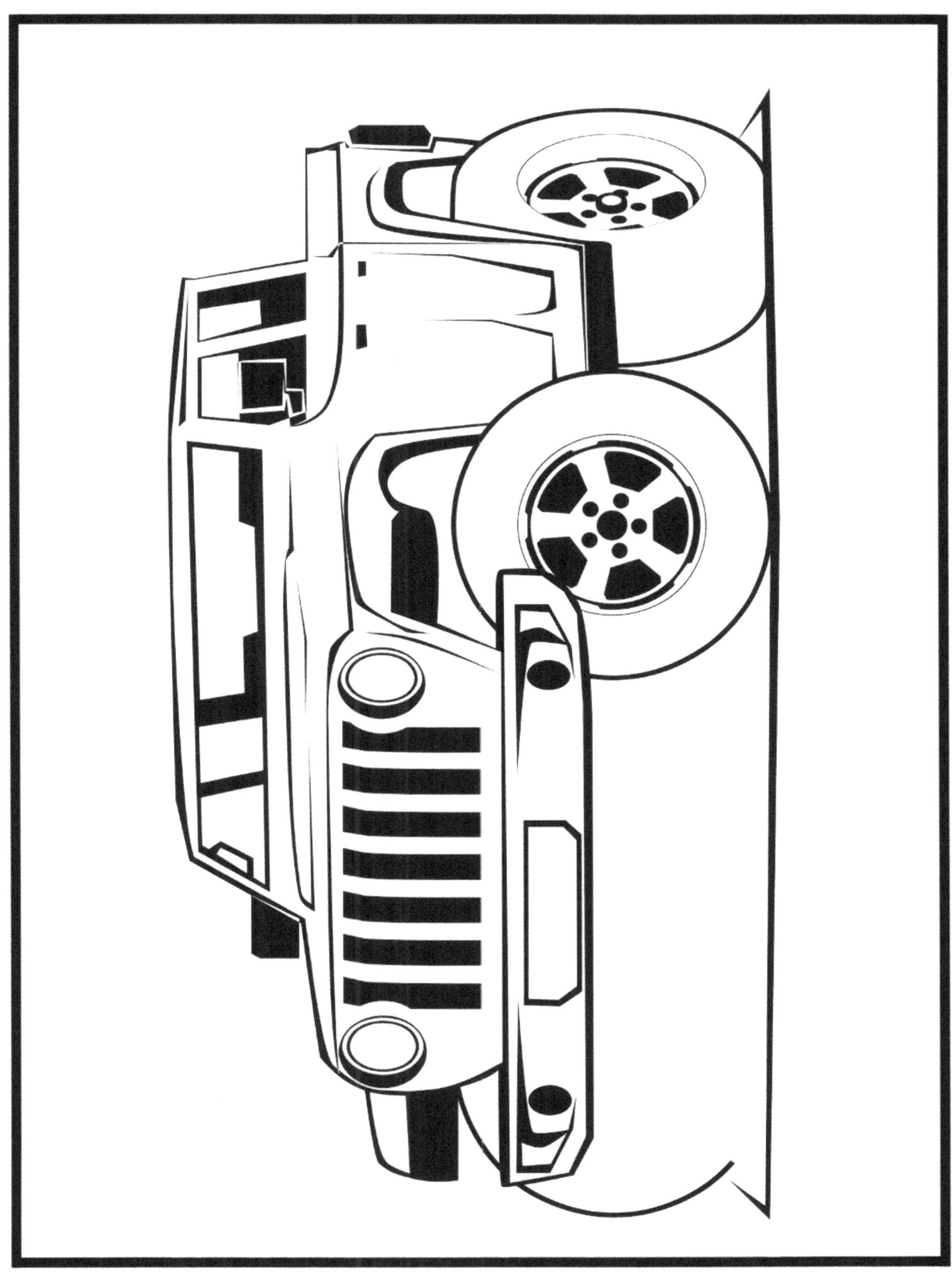

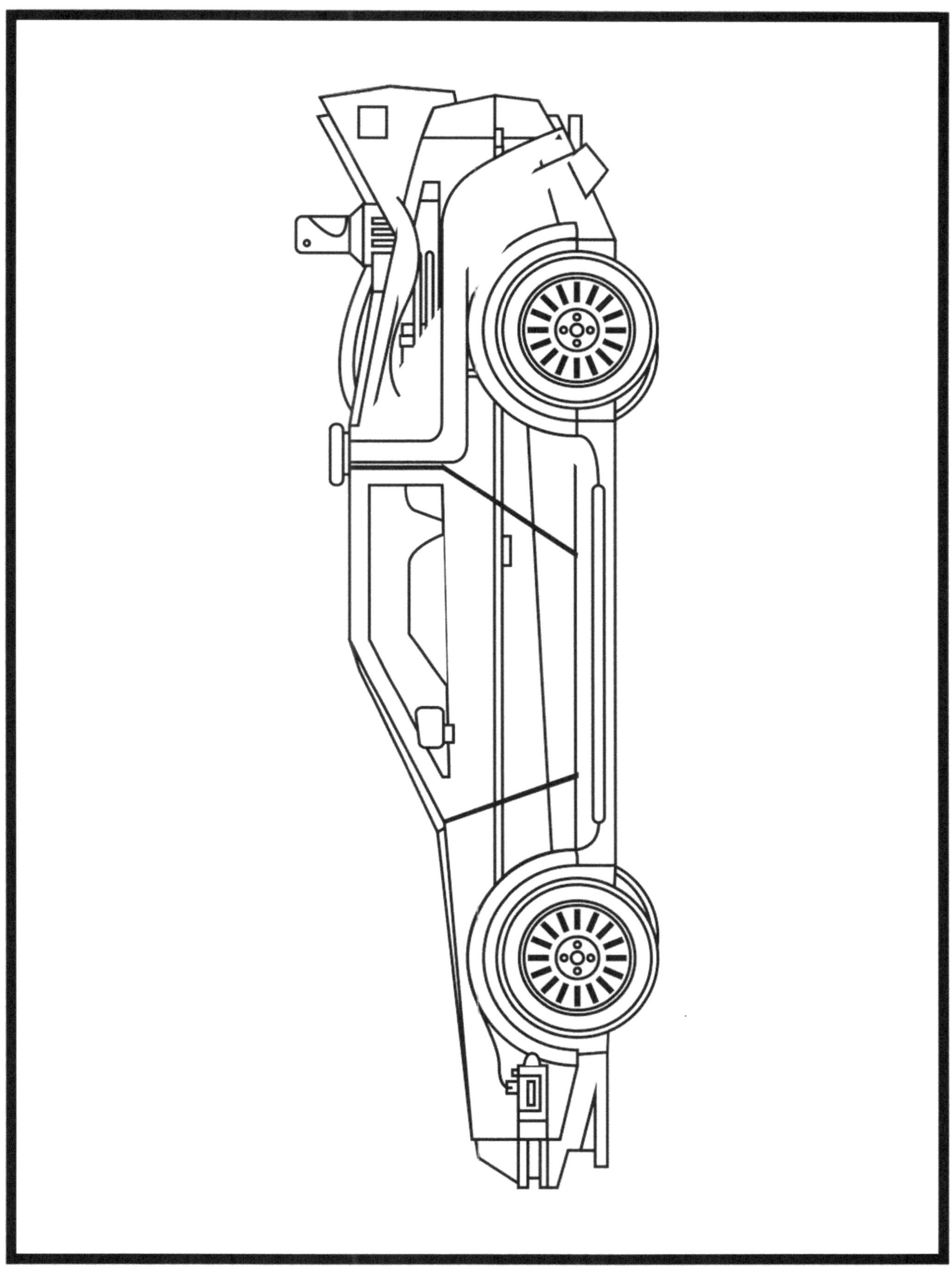

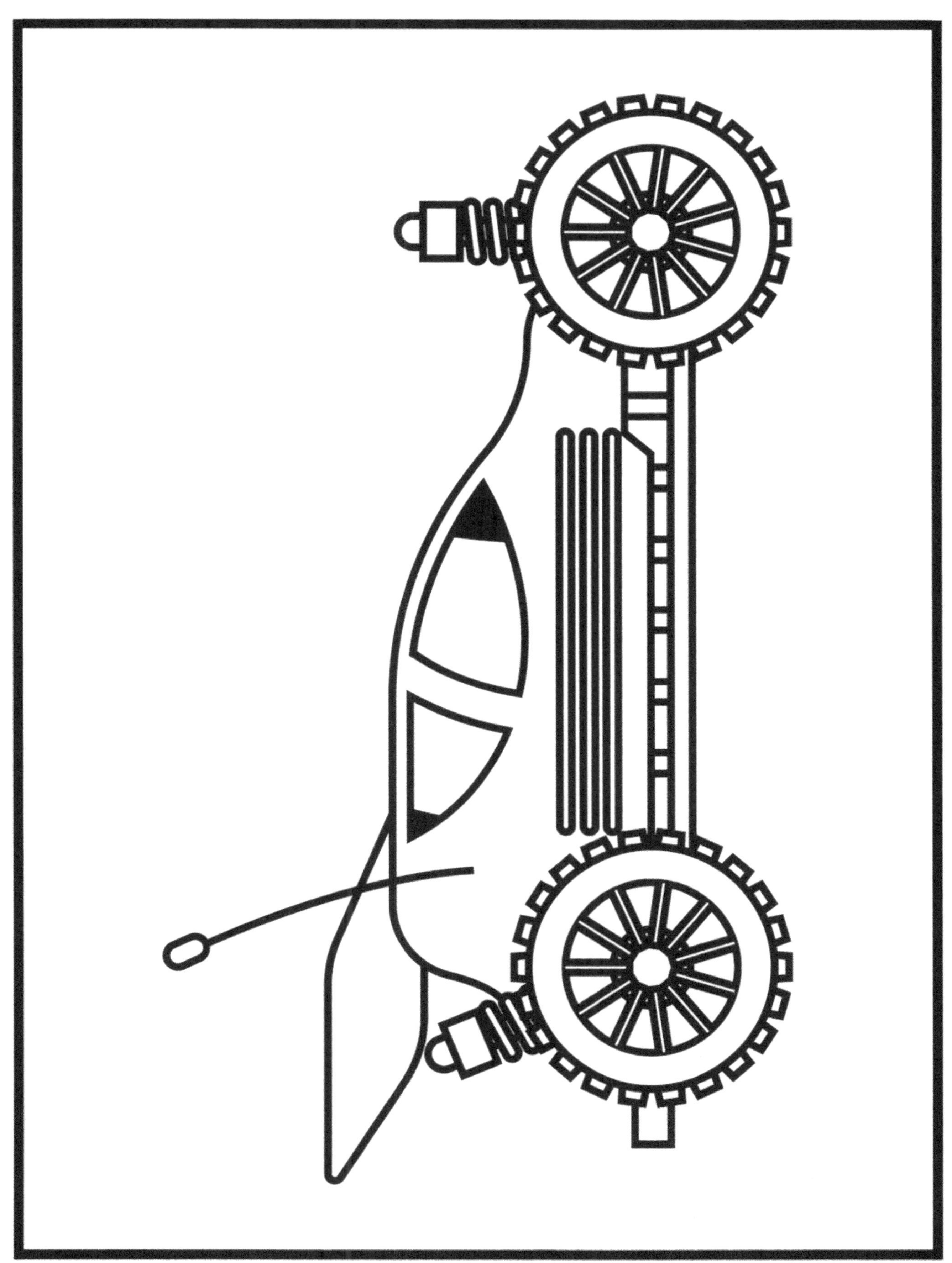

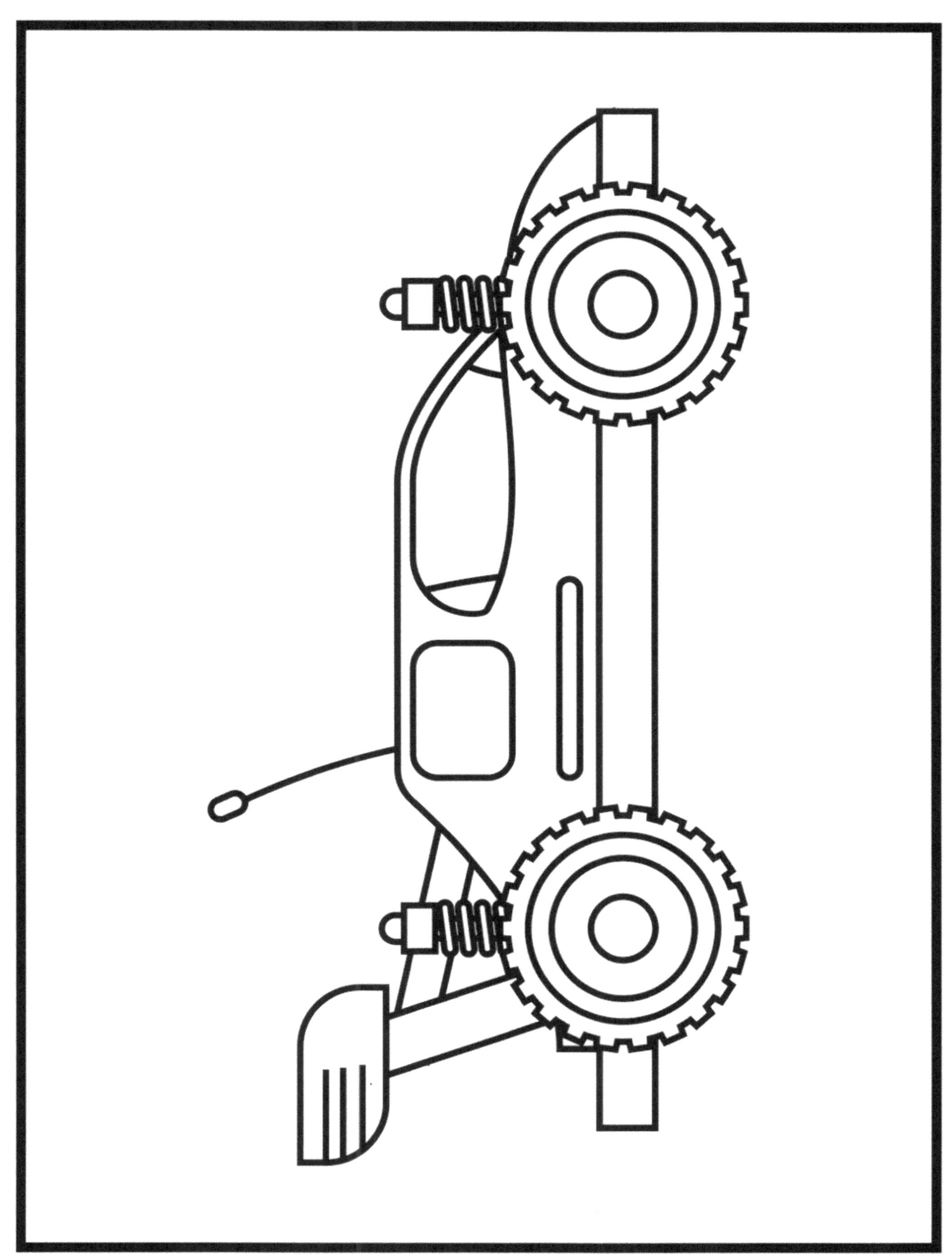

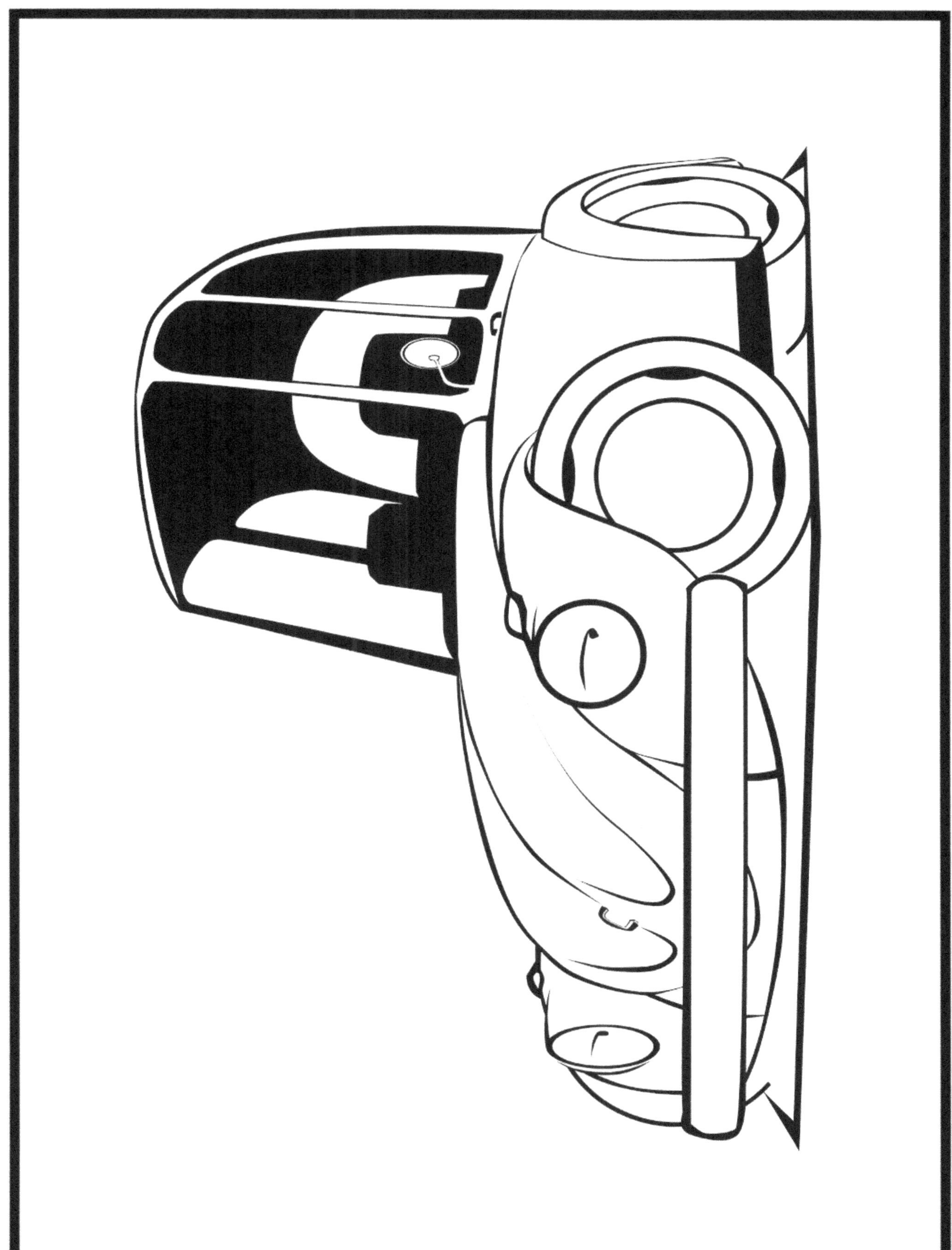

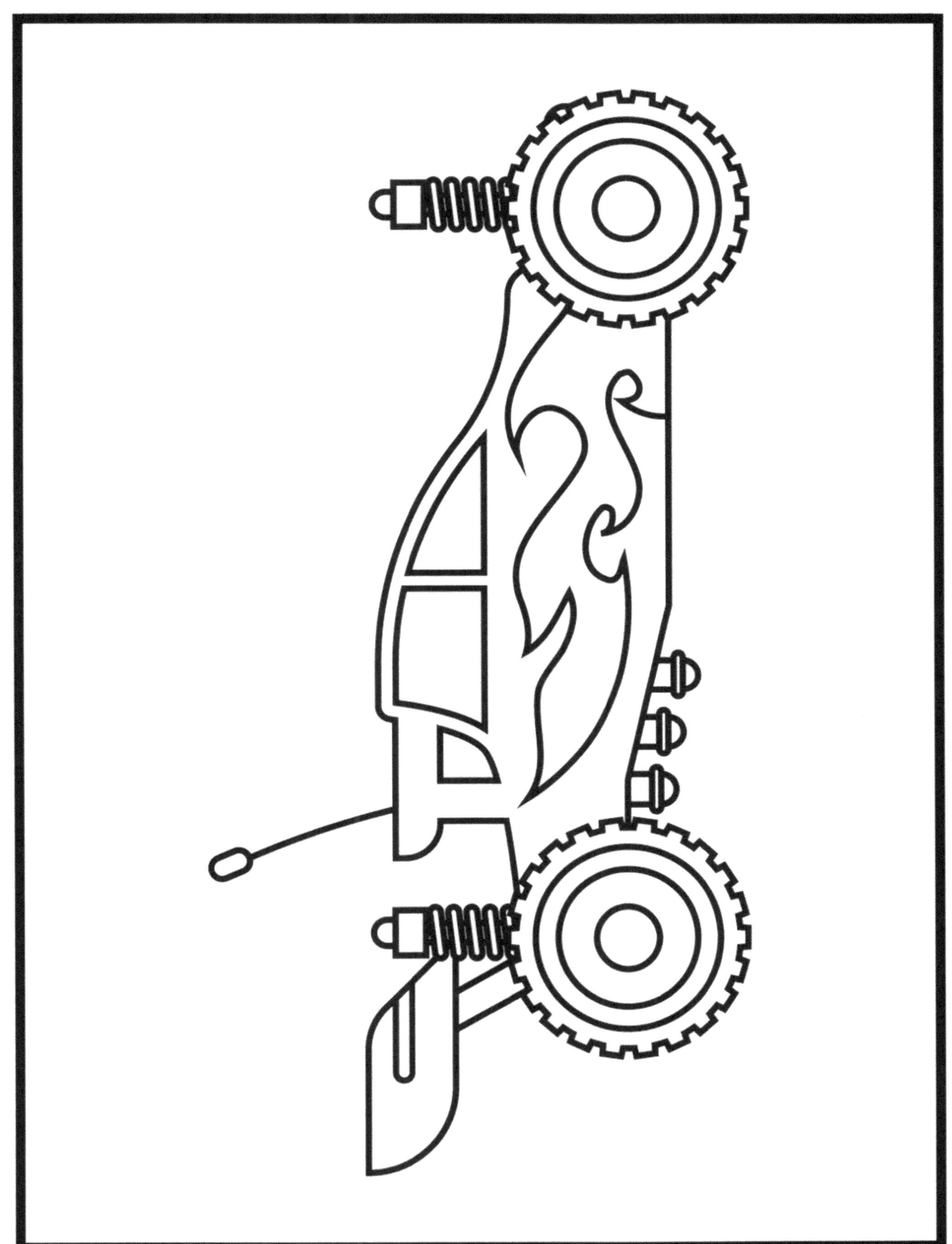

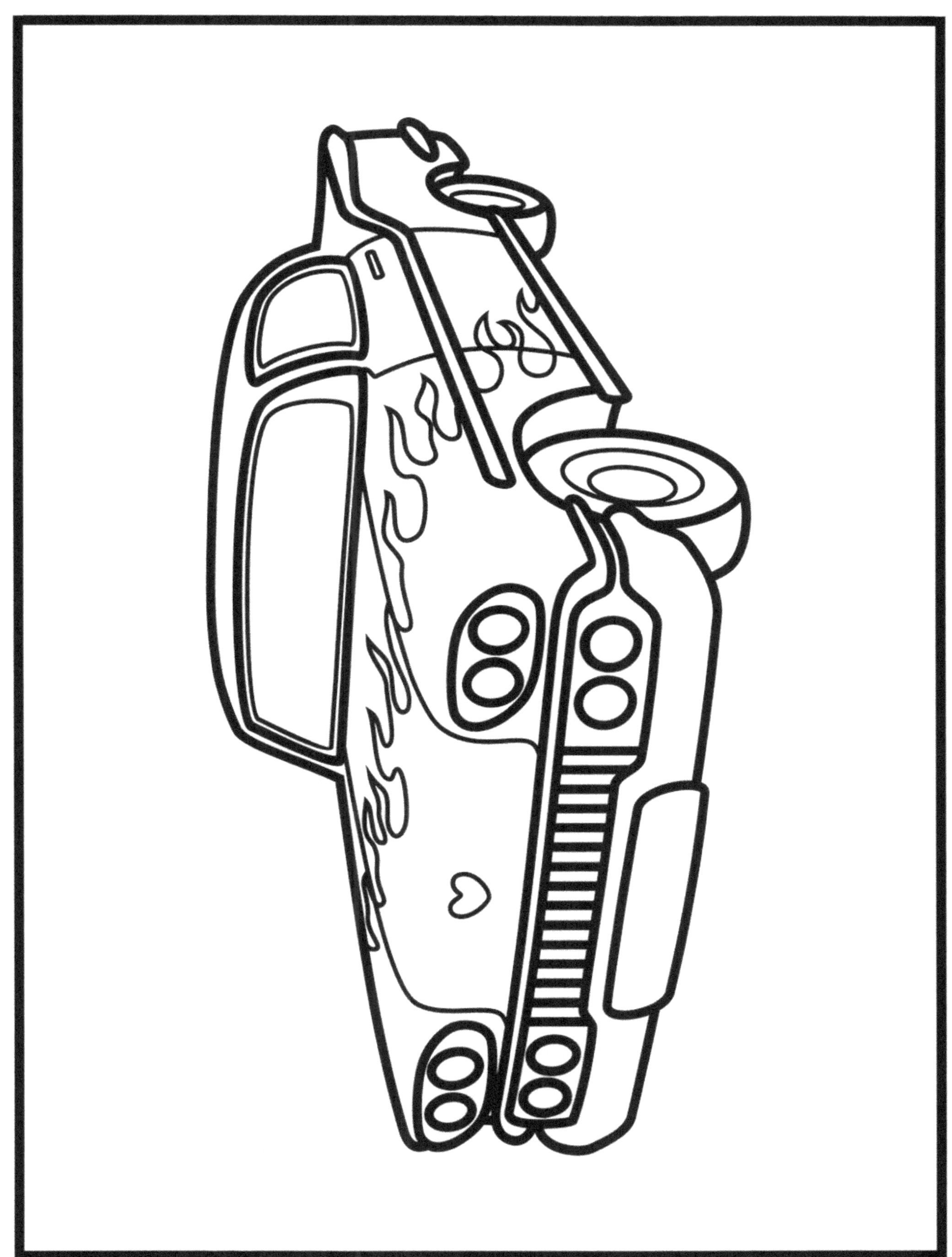

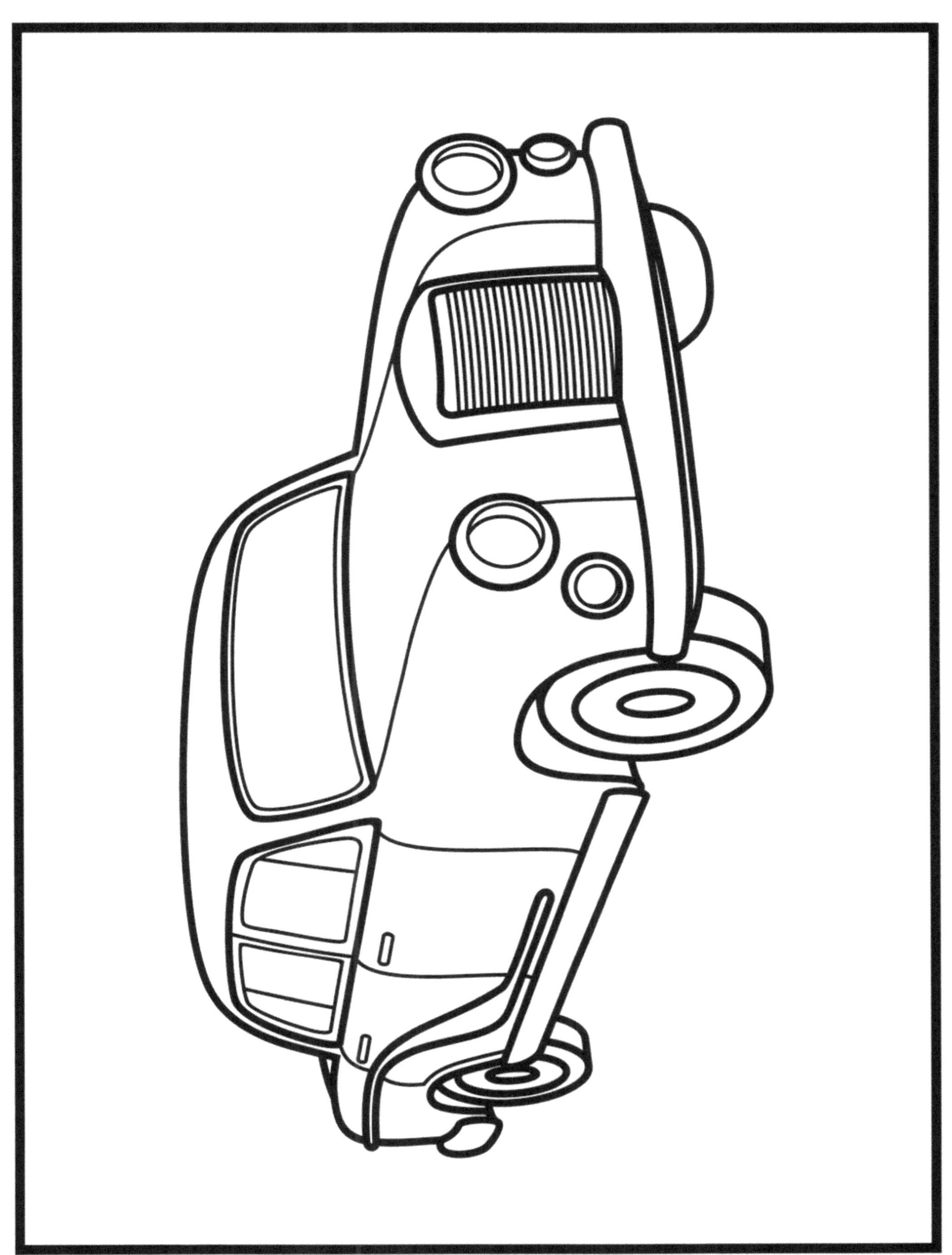

SS
SS

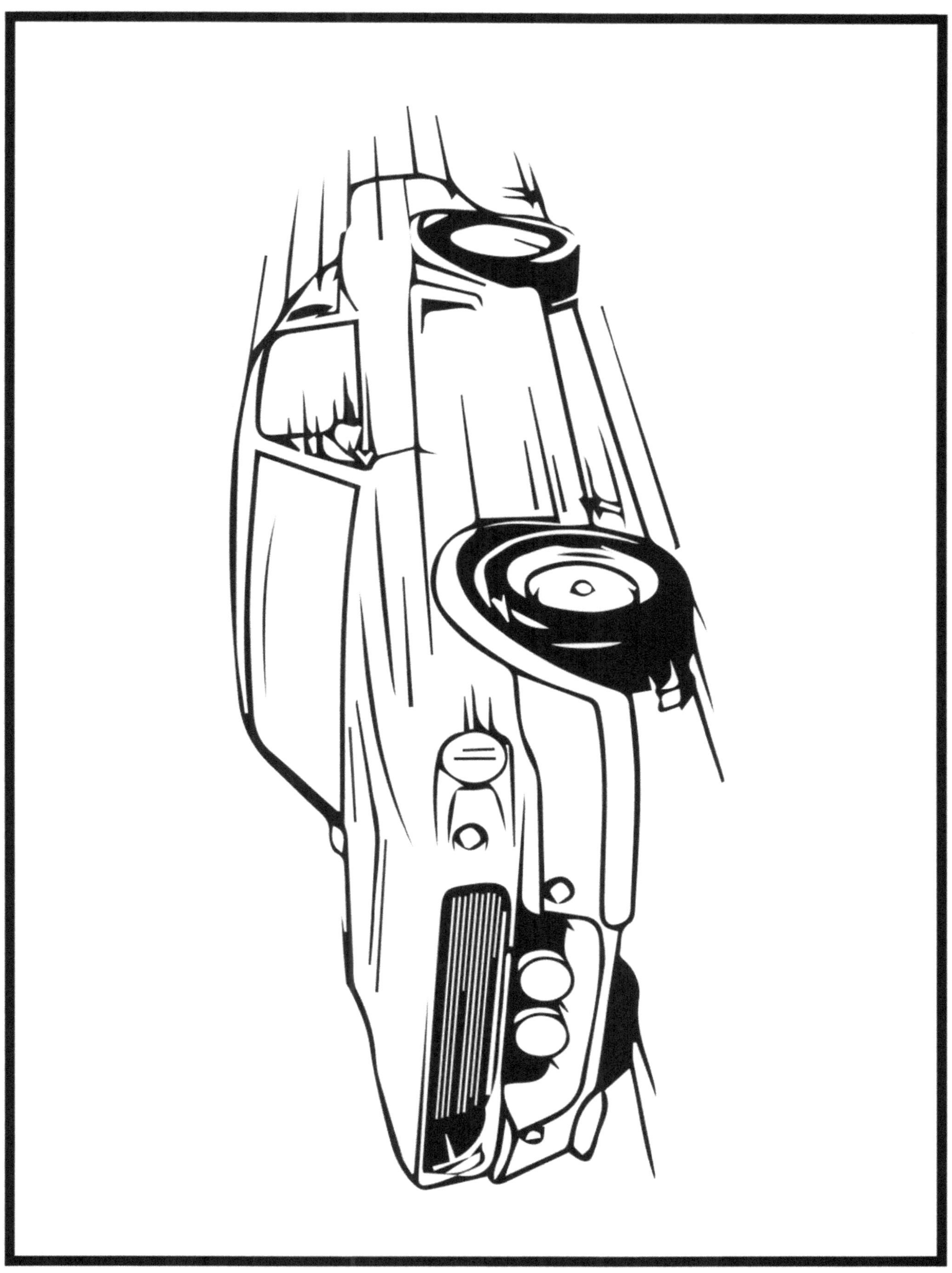

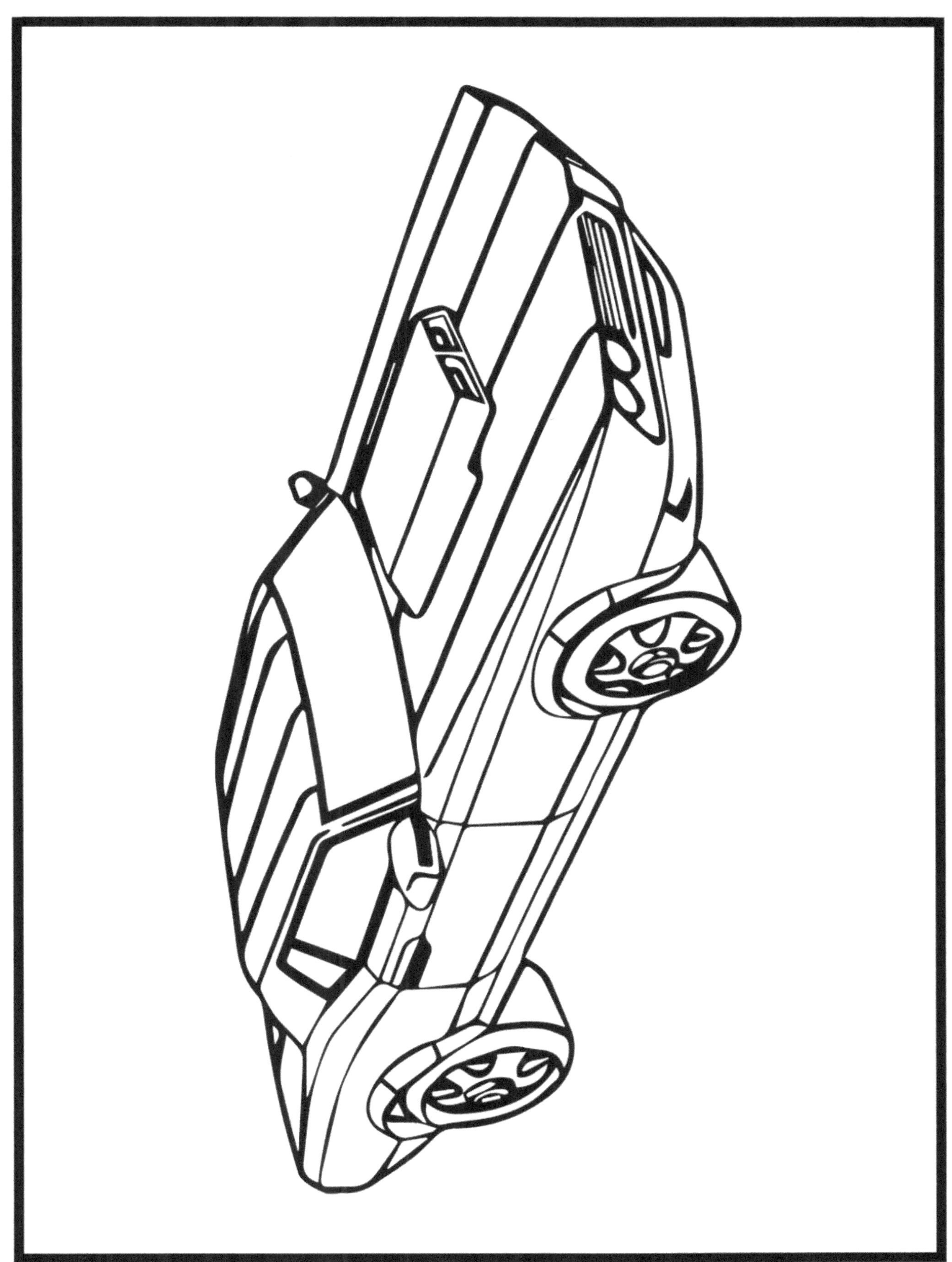

01

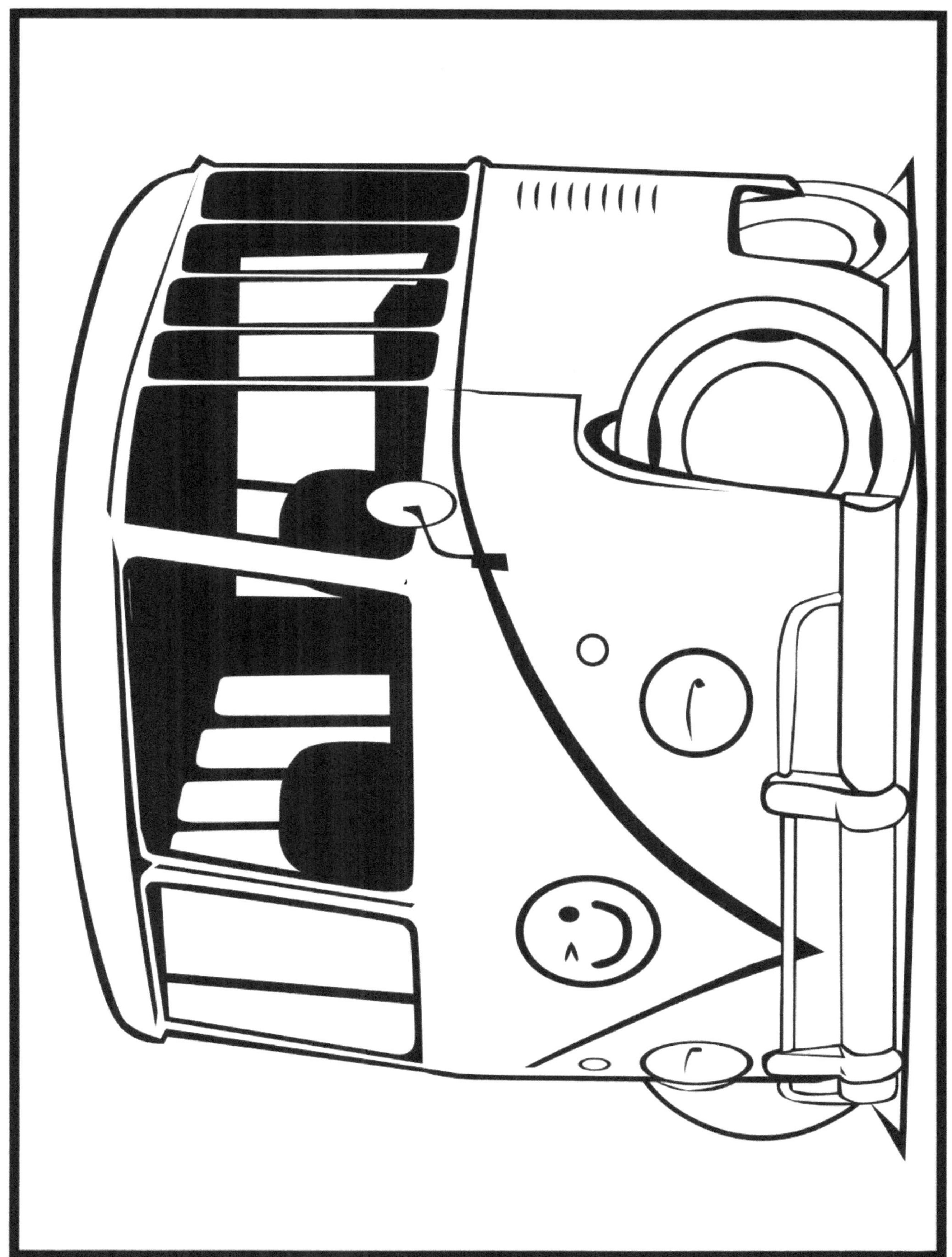

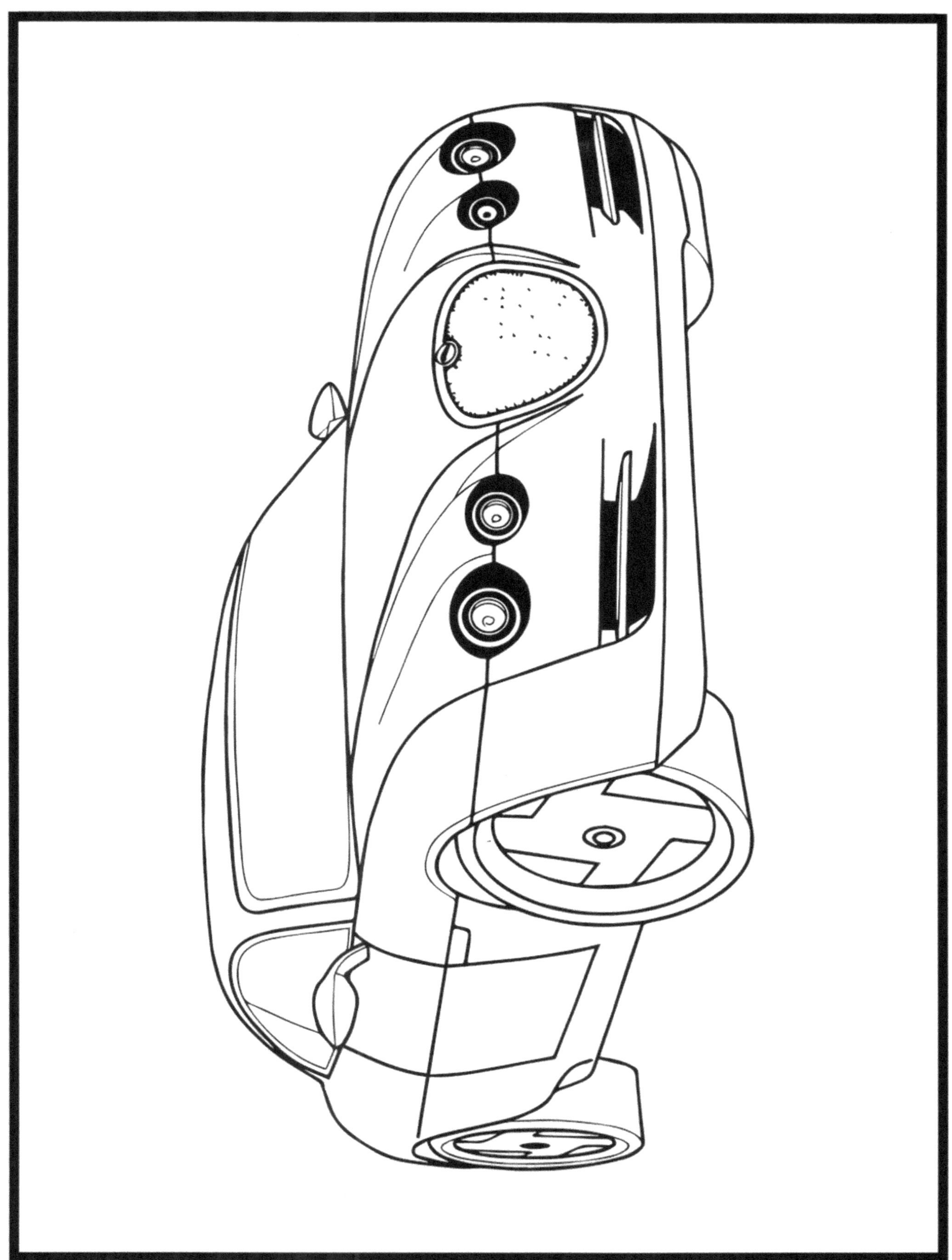

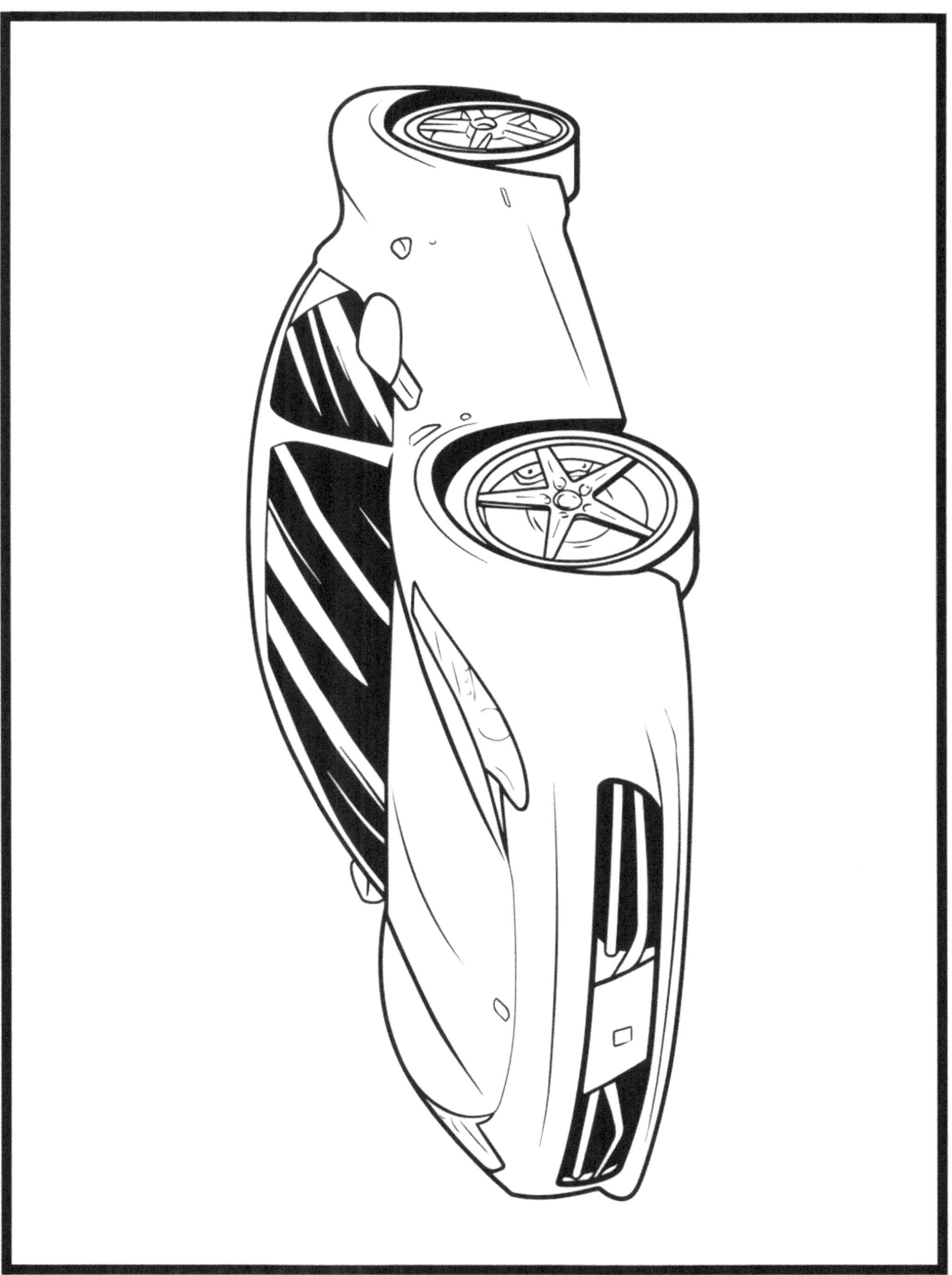

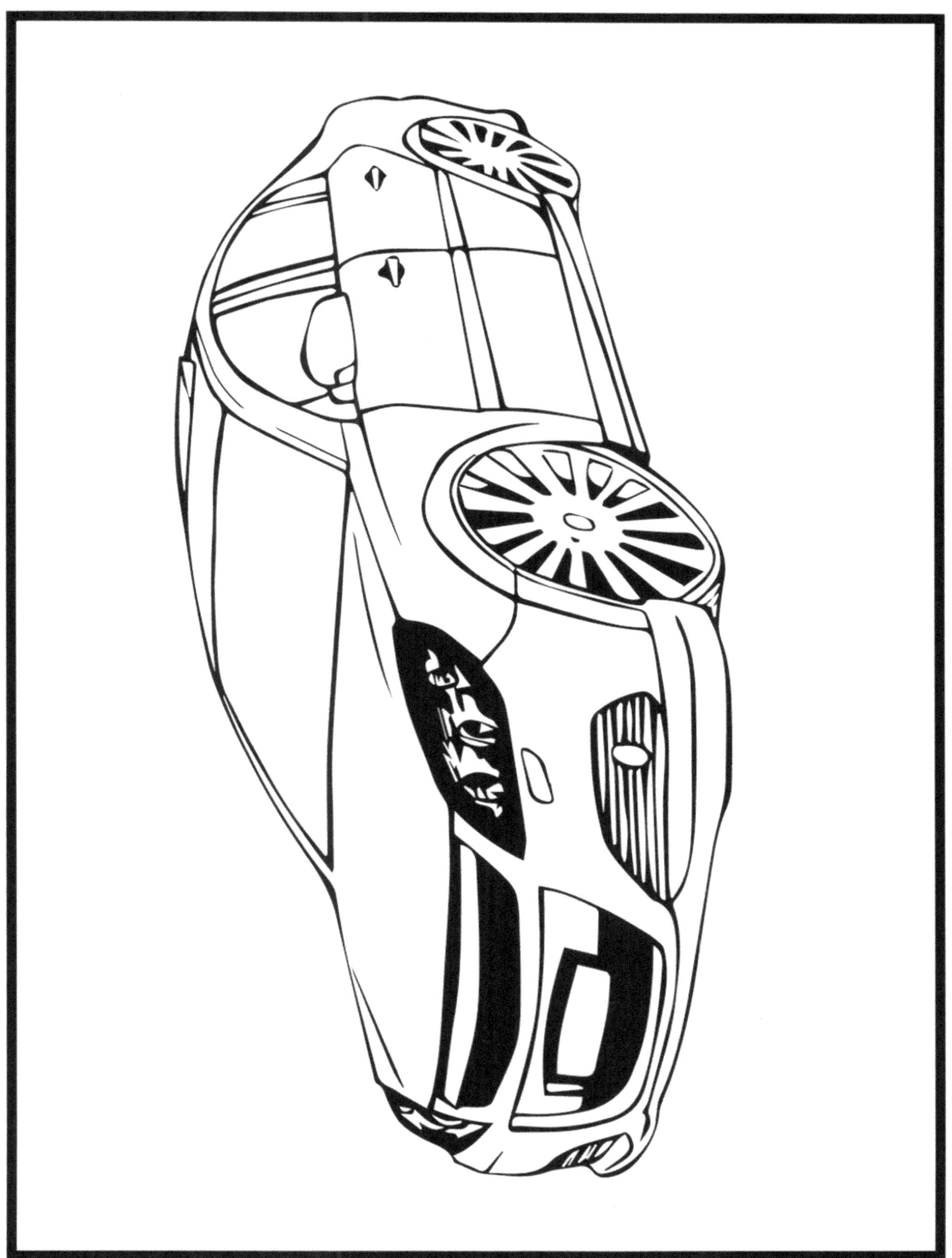

PEARL

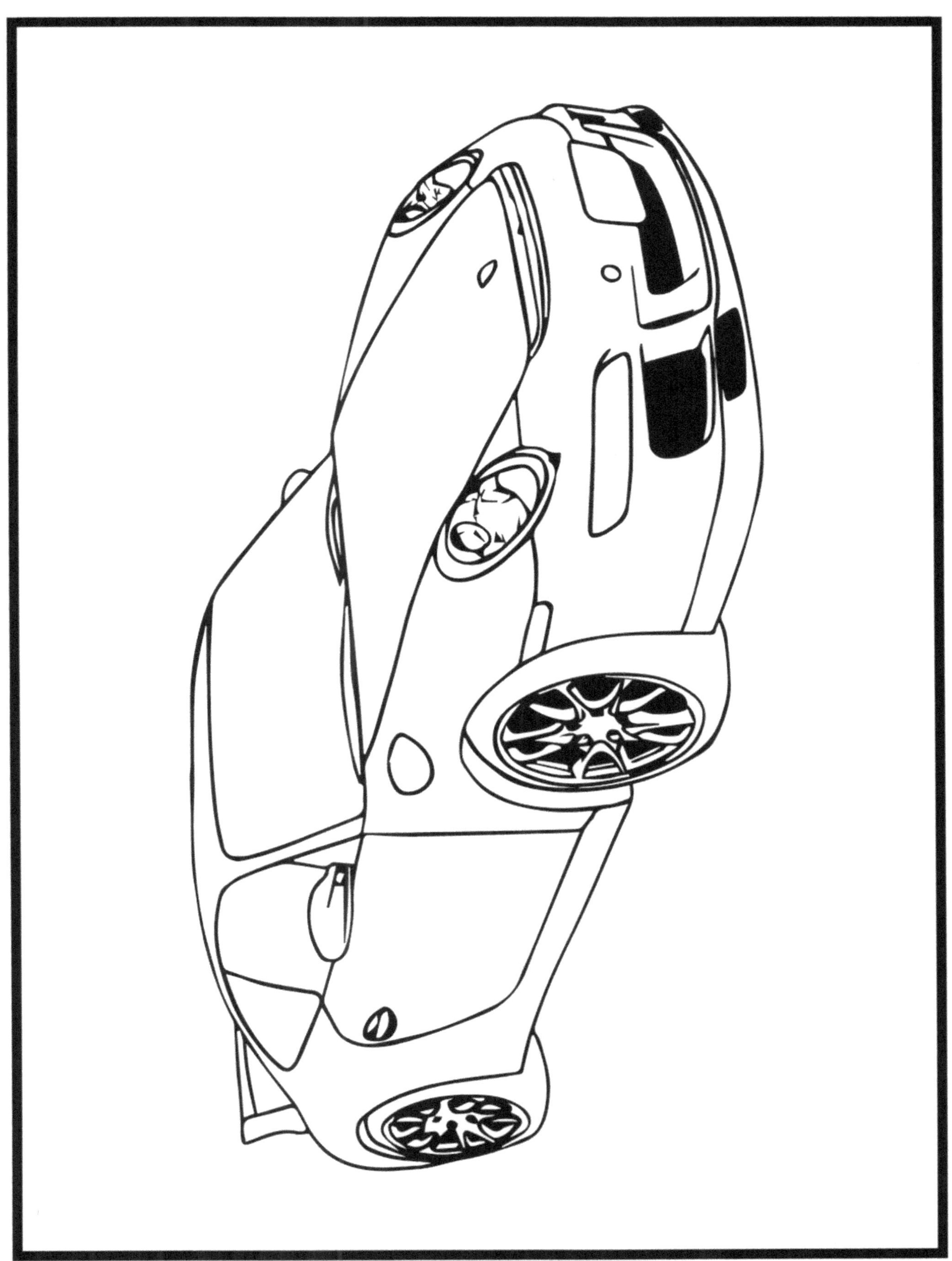

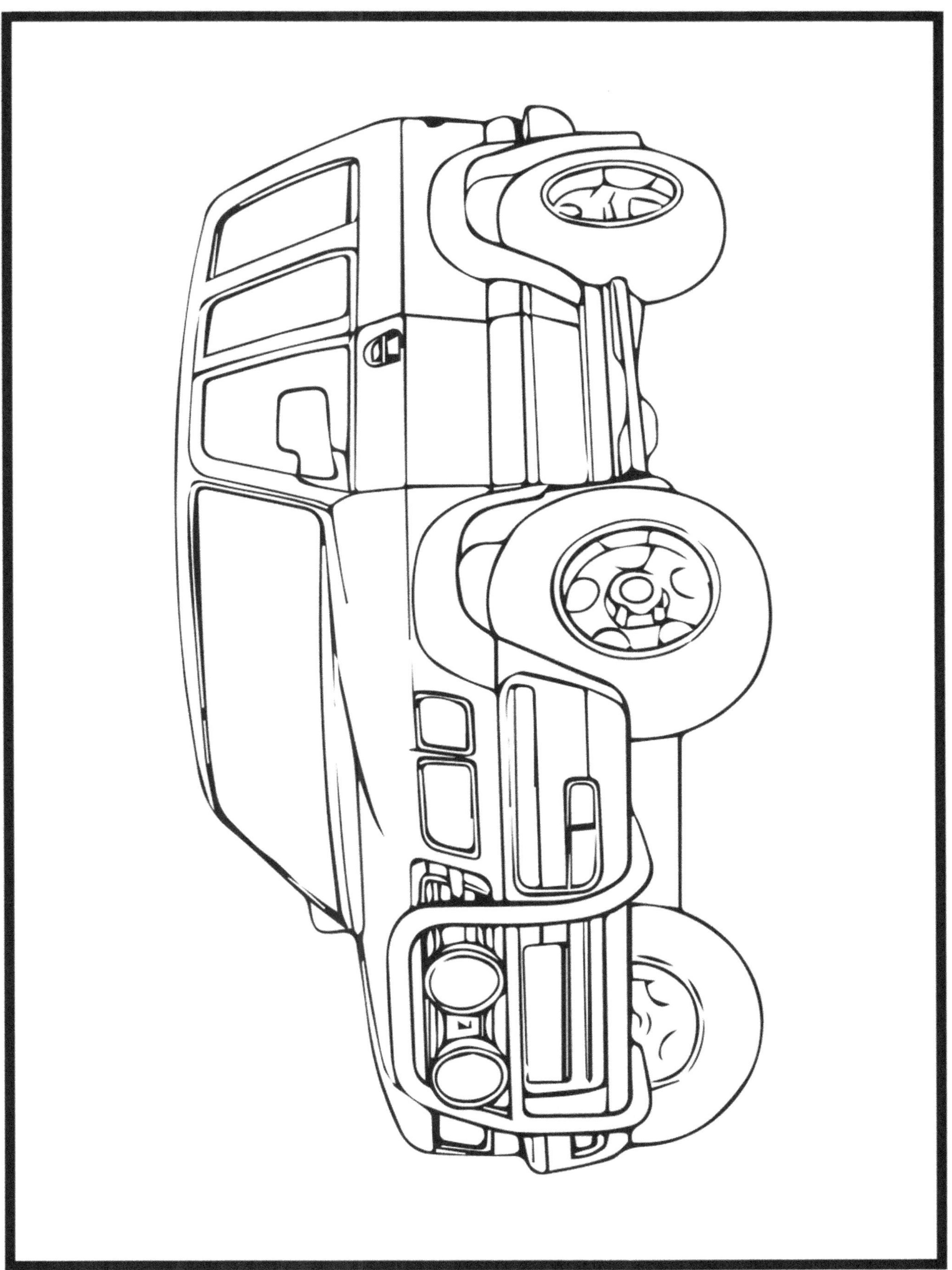

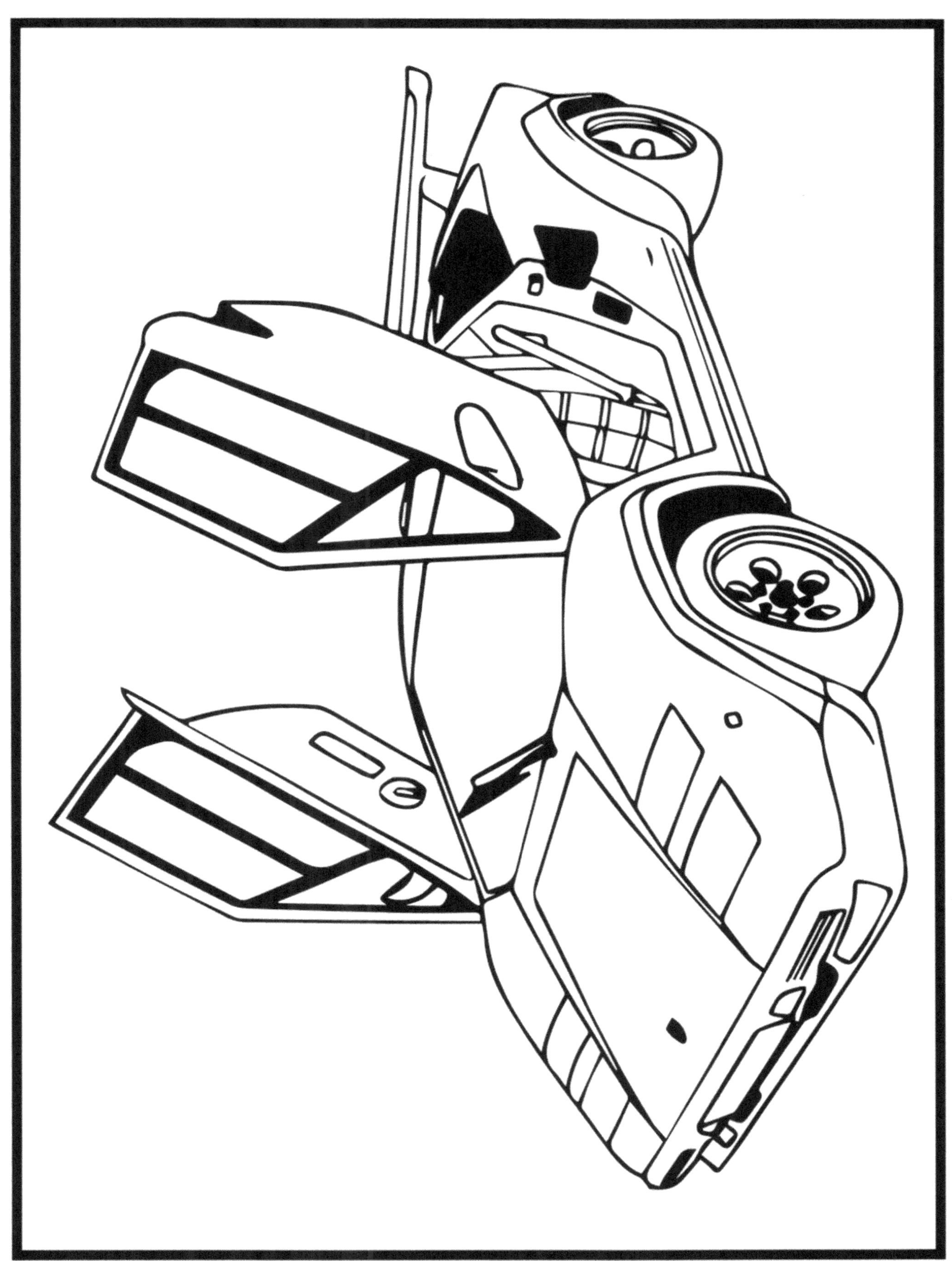

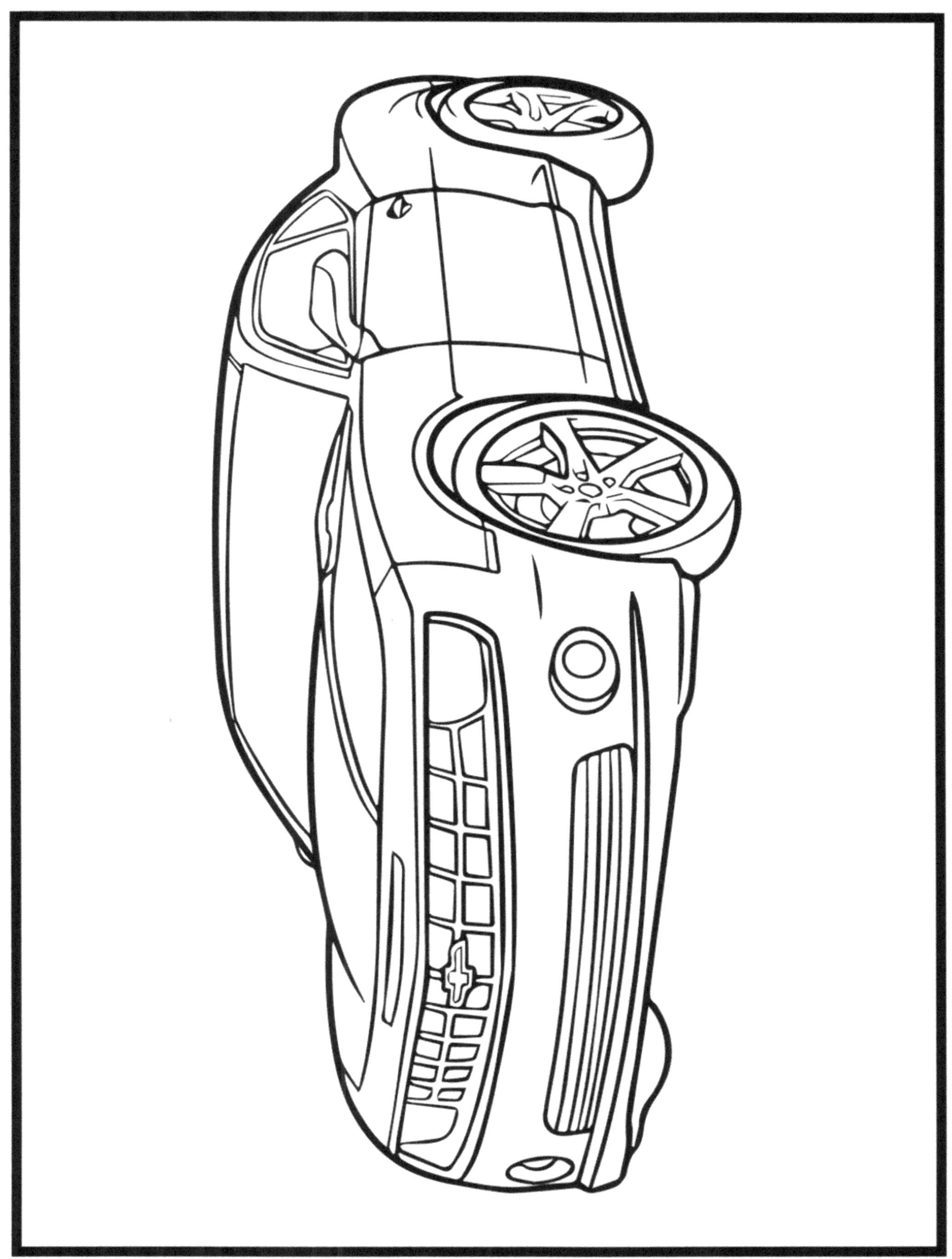

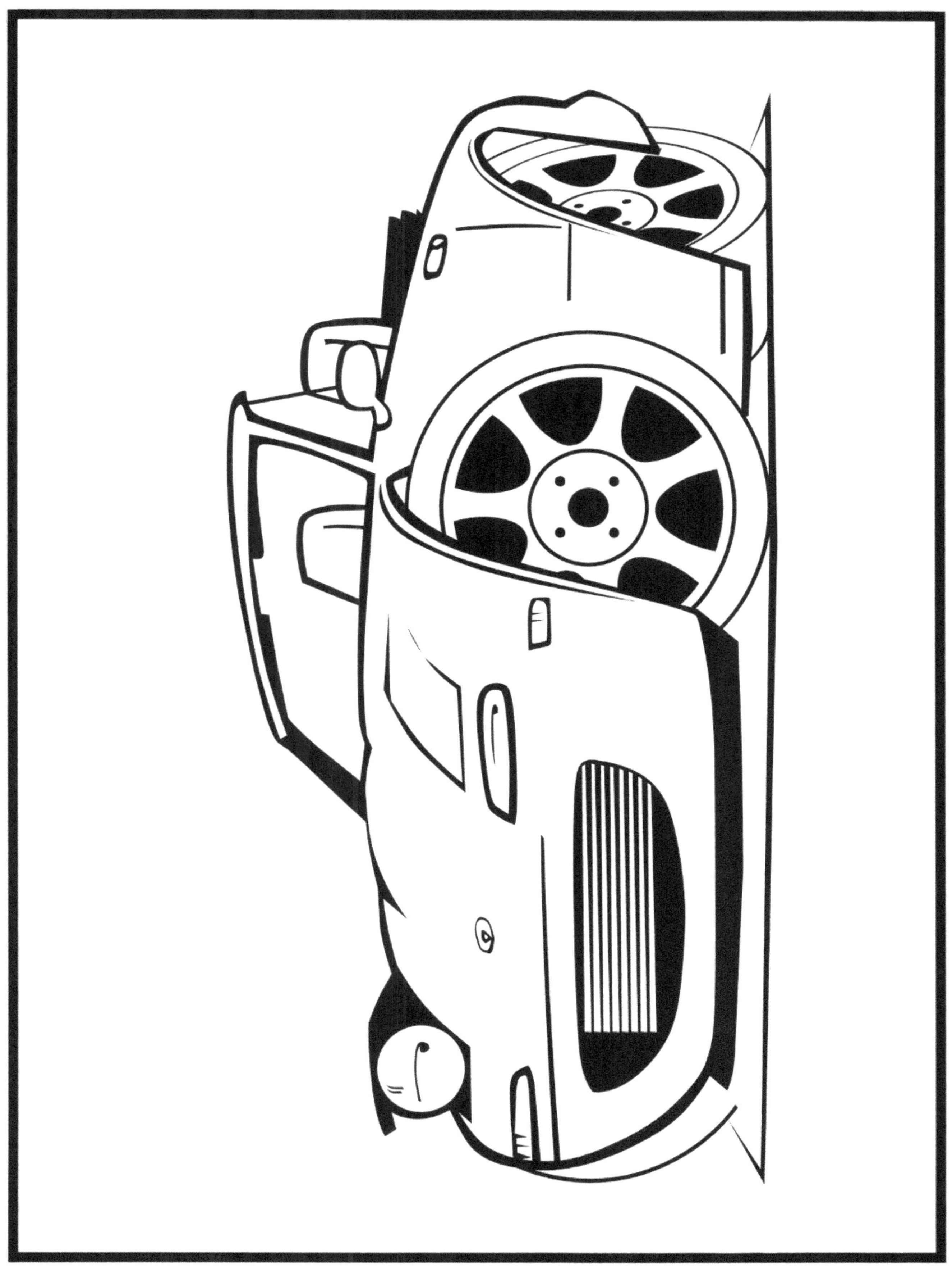

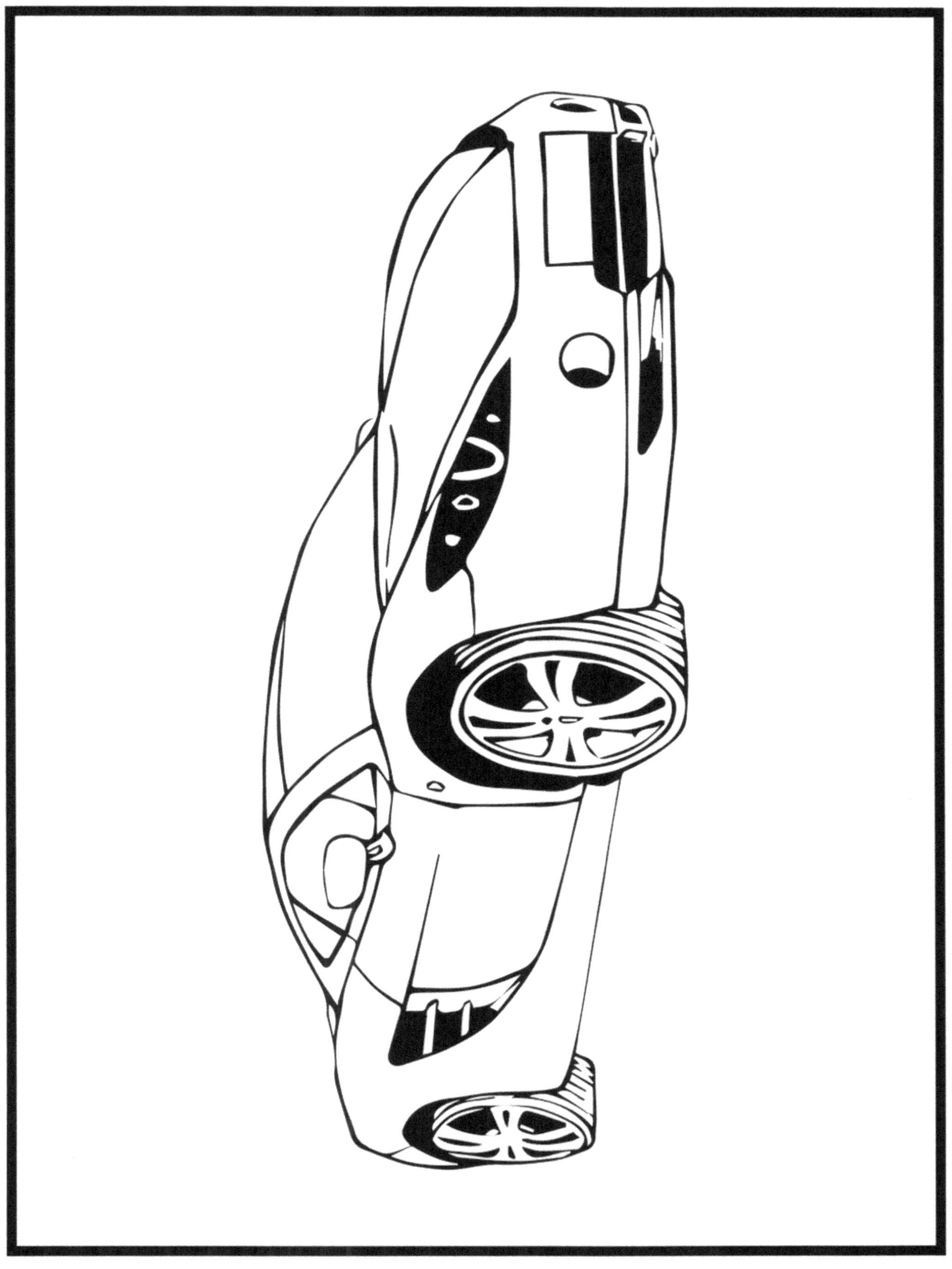

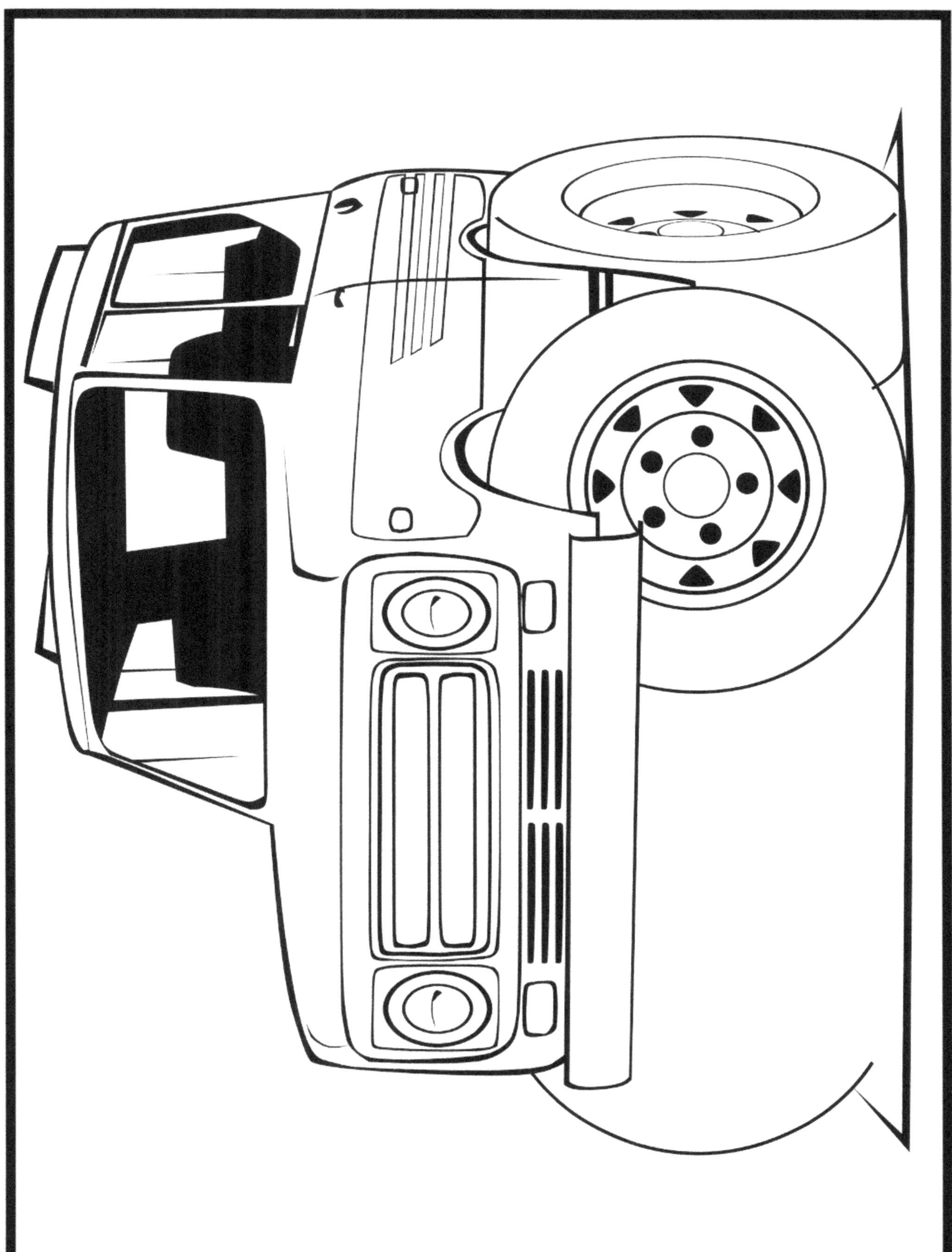

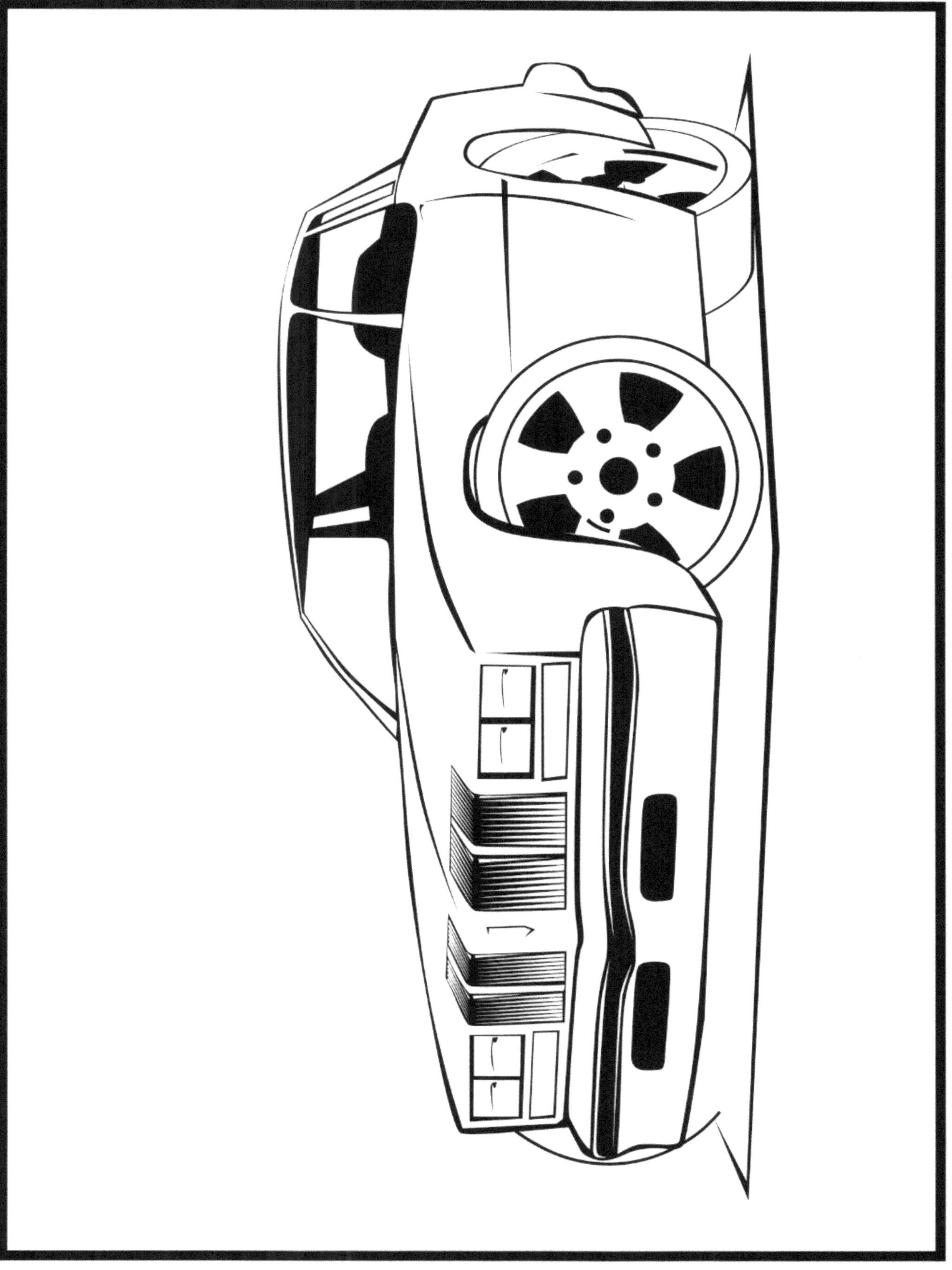

DESOTO
M69

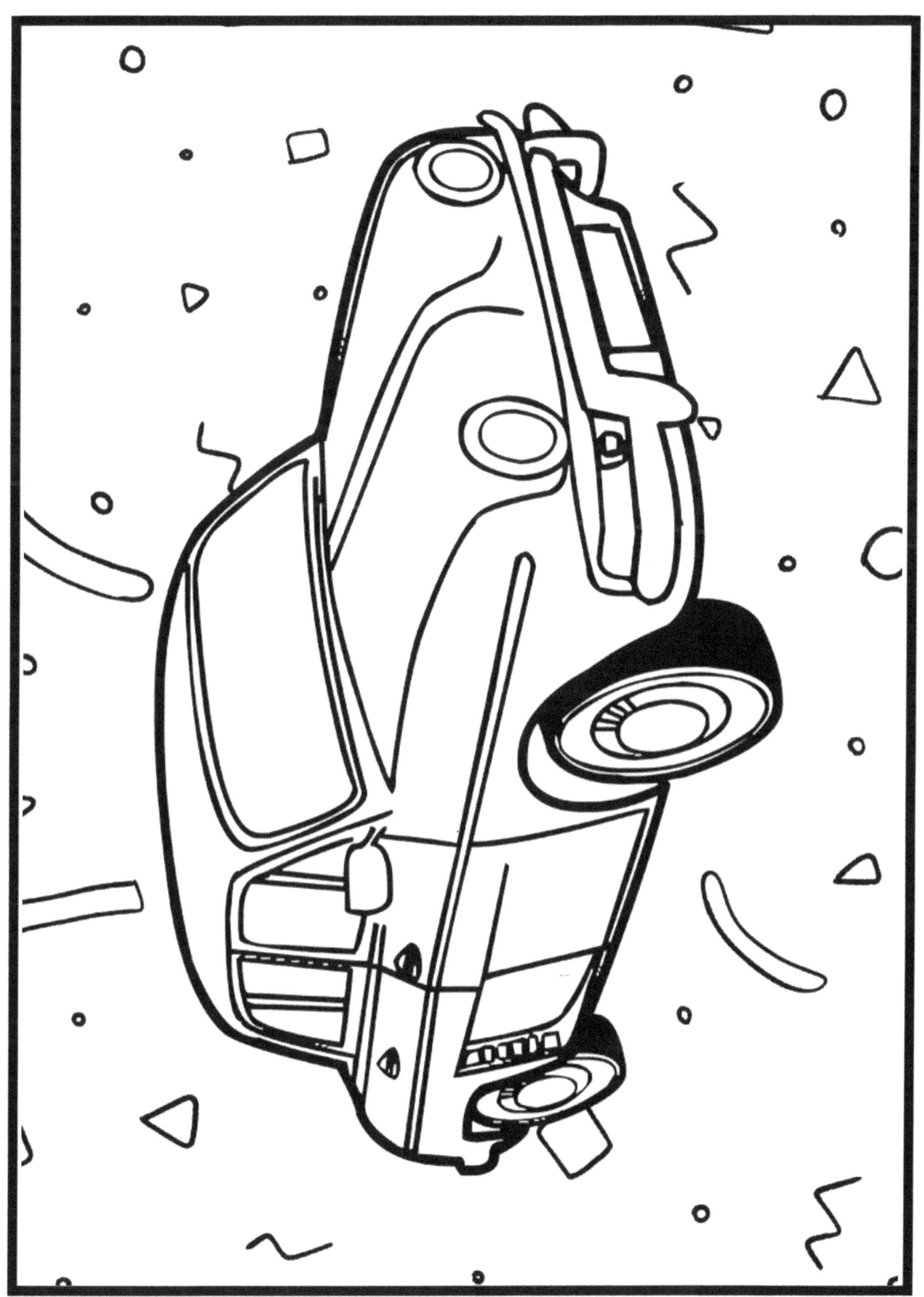

THANK YOU.

We hope that your kid has had many hours
of fun with our book and liked it
as much as we enjoyed working on it.

Your feedback
is very important to us.

Please let us know how you like our book at:
davina.claire.morgan@gmail.com

/davinaclairemorgan

/davinaclairemorgan